NO ONE ASKED FOR THIS

no one asked for this

musings during a global pandemic

NATALIE MARIA JOSE BLARDONY

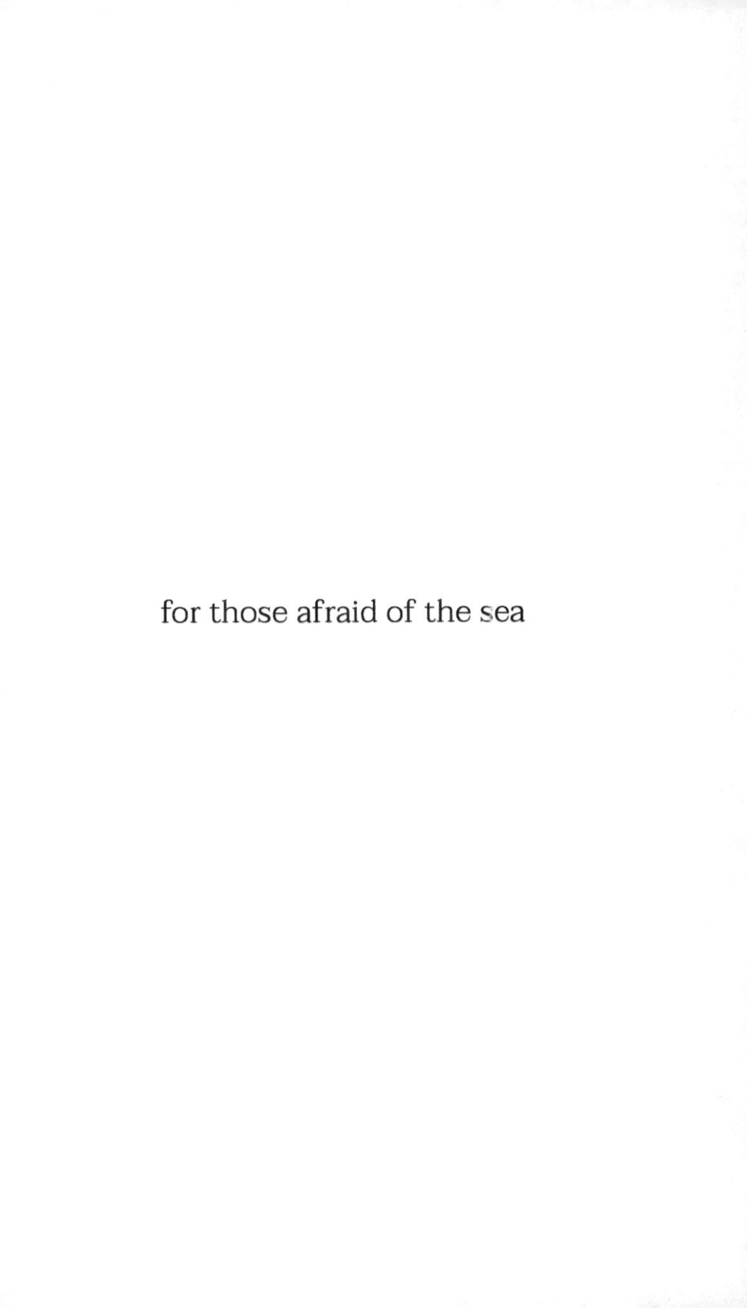

for those afraid of the sea

collections

the "i wish i didn't remember that god-
damn apartment" collection

the "i don't want to go without you"
collection

the "you will always be safe with me"
collection

the "she had something to say"
collection

intro

2020 started strong. I'm not the first to recognize the downward fall that happened since those early months of bliss. Ignorance in a world on fire.

But what the time since then has forced me into is a reflection I'm sure so many of you have also found yourselves trapped in. A retrospection you never asked for. Memories dug up from the recesses of your mind.

Happy tears. Heavy tears. Losing your breath. Catching your breath. Heart swelling, breaking.

The person we are forced to come face-to-face with when there's nothing else in the way to distract us from a reflection we've often tried to break.

At least that's how I felt. (Feel).

So I searched through my journals, my notepads, my phone to find the words that could help me make sense of the memories flooding my mind.

And what I found was a collection of all the times in my life that were forcing themselves upon me now. A series of poems and essays. Words from the darkest and brightest parts of myself. Words I didn't ask for.

Words that could give me some solace in a world too quiet, too loud. Too everything.

I didn't want this retrospection but it's actually

helped push me down a path of healing I always knew I needed but could never truly find.

And if nothing else, I'm glad I'm still moving forward. With you. Together.

i wish i didn't remember
that goddamn apartment

Chapter One

Fear.

Fear has been injected into my veins ever since I learned that people aren't what they seem.

Ever since I saw him take her behind closed doors and heard the screaming stop.

Ever since I saw them emerge, more broken than before.

Fear coats my tongue. It colors everything I taste. The night I used to love suffocates me to a near death each time I step into it.

Safety.

I want to be wrapped in its warmth. I don't want to be strangled or held down. I don't want to watch the volume of my words or my music.

I want a comforter snuggled tight around my

shoulders. I want frivolous thoughts falling in and out of my head. I want laughter so strong it throws my head back into the sofa holding me close.

I thought I had that. That after all these years I'd finally built a home that felt like the one I'd been searching for all my 28 years.

But it's funny how quickly that can change, isn't it? Nowhere is safe it seems. Not the place birthed from blood or the place built from it. Everywhere is just waiting to be destroyed.

I'm so tired of that. Of this anxious panic hanging over my head. This fucking guillotine just waiting to drop. Why can't I seem to dismantle that? Take it away and trash this ancient torture device.

Why is everything just happening no matter how hard we try to stop it?

I've skinned my hands so many times I doubt I even have fingerprints anymore.

But still, still it happens.

Chapter Two

I never used to be able to remember much
of that day, that night. This greyness is what
has always stopped me from saying more but
the further I am from those days, that place,
the more I do remember. The more I feel my
voice returning to my mouth. My strength to
my veins.

I've sewn so much doubt into the facts of
my life that I don't even think I'd be a reliable
witness for myself. It's taken years to remove
their voices from my head and the narrative
they've built, that now my own sometimes
takes on their words for them.

It's like they never left.

But the fog is starting to lift and a story is
piecing itself together in real-time. I'm terrified

of seeing the final picture but it's too late to stop this.

The memories are coming and I can't do anything but barricade myself from them.

Steady my stance.

Stiffen my upper lip.

Do I even want to know everything that my mind has protected me from? Do I want to look at my body and see their hands instead of mine?

Chapter Three

I close my eyes and peel the skin off my body. See the layers come off, gentle and smooth. Satisfying.

The flesh melting away from my fat. So much fat.

It melts between my fingers, ice cream on a day hotter than I've felt in months.

Plastic over an open flame.

Why don't I feel anything?

I open my eyes, touch myself to see if the fantasies I dreamt came to fruition.

Instead, I still feel something to grab, something to squeeze. Nothing comes off as easy as it should. Here, in this bed, in this room, it clings to me like superglue.

I pull, harder, harder,

"Why won't you let go?"
    I'm scared. Too scared.
"No one wants you."

I close my eyes again, preferring that to the world that surrounds me, and feel the cool of the knives cutting into my seams. A relief too sweet to forget.

One day, one day
I'll do something.
Do something to change this hell.
Turn it on its head.
Show her what I can do,
show them what I'm worth.
One day.

Chapter Four

I thought I was done.

Done with these muffled tears and silent cries.

I don't understand why I'm still stuck in this rut.

This weight,
> a permanent leech on my soul,
it's drowning me.

I'm so tired of fighting.

Chapter Five

I felt the sting in the back of my throat,
the bile still hugging my tongue.
Listerine was never enough.
What was the best way to get rid of acid?
I tried to fold into the conversation happen-
ing around me,
but it was always harder after seeing him.
His voice was too much, "You wouldn't taste
that if you finished.
If you did what we came here for."
"You wouldn't feel what you do now if you
just listened."
"Just listen to me."
"Listen to me."
"Listen."

Chapter Six

I used to hate food. Only a few years ago did I spend countless hours huddled around the only thing I thought loved me.

Digging my nails so deep into my side, I still have some scars to show those brave enough to look into a past I'm too ashamed of. Or maybe I'm not ashamed anymore? Maybe I'm just scared that if I look too closely I'll still see parts of that self in myself today.

See the girl who couldn't walk into a Panera without spinning out of control. Grasping desperately to the fat on her bones so she could keep her feet steady.

This world always seemed to move too fast. I didn't know what I wanted but in as fast as it took to burn, I realized that my life was already decided.

In the deepest hours of the night, I'd get up and stumble into the bathroom. Groggy, uncertain of the shadows creeping alongside me. I tried as hard as I could to avert my eyes from the reflection but each night I caught a glimpse of a future I knew was waiting for me. I saw something I wanted alongside everything I didn't. I saw a future drowning in toxins I didn't want to have inside of me anymore.

I saw him standing there. His arms plastered against my skin. Turning the brown into a white so translucent I began to bleed. The color in my face draining with each second we stayed together. The life I'd feel from the job I imagined for myself would be drained the moment I saw him. The moment I saw any of those hims. I saw those eyes, her eyes, begging me to take control while I could.

But that was too much to deal with. Too much for my seventeen-year-old mind to handle. Not when I was getting assigned engagement projects by our Religion teacher in high school. Literally writing my future into existence. Picking a senior quote for the yearbook from the song we called ours once upon a time. Plastering memories of high school with a boy I knew would never make it out of this alive.

I wasn't going to make it out of this alive.

I wasn't sure when, but I felt death creeping closer. By no one's hand but my own. I began to fantasize about that day. Wonder what it'd feel like to be free of this suffocation. What it'd feel like to just jump off the ledge I always felt pulled away from. I know I didn't have wings and I couldn't fly but would that really kill me? More than the life I was living then?

So I buried myself in a mountain of distractions so tall they came crashing down. Brick by brick, I piled them on top of me. Desperate for something else to focus on. And then it came, the feel of my stomach rolling on top of my jeans. The sight of my thighs touching one another. The lack of the collar bone in pictures. The jokes from loved ones. The jeans that were now too small. The shirts that hugged parts I didn't want. The dress zippers that broke. The toes I couldn't see in the shower.

This was the issue. This was the real problem here. This was something I could control. If I just finished this week-long fast, that would be enough. That would get me a few pounds closer. That would push me closer to a finish line where at least one thing would be okay. A life where I'd at least have the body of my dreams even if I couldn't have my dream. If I had to live this lie and feel myself disintegrate in the fire I set in my chest, I'd at least look damn good on the outside.

The endless string of ways to expunge the meals I'd eat, scarf away, was something I couldn't figure out how to quit. It was the love affair I never had. The one I had always wanted. The passion, the fire. The on-off relationship. One second it seemed to hate me, make me hate me. Break the mirrors in hopes of cutting myself apart.

The next, we were in a heated tango. Tangled up within each other's love. They'd tell me sweet nothings, whisper them into my hair the morning after. It was always this hot and cold type of thing. There was nothing stable but then again what else in life was?

And then the most exciting part of all: secrecy. The hush-hush nature of us. It kept the fire burning, the sexy alive. "No one can ever know," he'd whisper. "Not even her. Especially not her."

Even as I lay on that floor, cold and shaking, he'd tell me that one day this would all be worth it. That he loved me and that he was the only one who ever would. That he was the saving grace I'd been praying for all those nights before. That this was the escape I so desperately craved. That despite what I was telling myself, he was the one keeping me alive.

I grew so used to this comfort, this destruction in one that I leaned on him for another ten years before I saw him for what he was.

But not before he took away so many parts I just want back.

So many parts I'm tired of hunting down.

So many parts I'll never find again.

Blood drained down the pipes of Boston College. Tears eating away at the memories.

I don't want that anymore.

I didn't really want it then.

I screamed so loud once, when no one was home. Careful that no one would hear. But so desperate for someone to listen. I screamed. With everything left in my lungs, I let it out. It was primal. Fulfilling. Terrifying.

It echoed in my ears and I remember how quickly he came running in. Quick to pull me into his arms. Rock me back and forth. Wiping the bile away from my lips, the sweat from my forehead. Singing sweet lullabies into my ears. He looked so kind in those moments. He felt so warm. Like he was the only one who could understand.

But then I'd be right back on my knees, purging out more and more until I couldn't see my reflection in the water anymore.

Because nothing was uglier than that. Nothing made me want to stop. Nothing gave me the energy I needed to push that tooth brush further and further back. Even if I heard her trying with the little voice she had to stop me. To pull that brush away from the fingers slipping on its rubber.

She was drowned out by him by tenfold. She didn't stand a chance without me wanting to give her one. I didn't want anything to do with her.

I wanted him and his distractions and his world of could-be-if-only-x. I wanted that fantasy he promised. The happily ever after he said we'd have together. I didn't want to have to start this all over with someone else. Re-examine the life I was running away from. Dig into the wounds I only made deeper, wider with every trip to the bathroom, with every sip of those drinks.

He was the only thing I knew I could count on. The only thing I could hold onto.

But thinking back to that time, I can see I wasn't holding onto him at all. I wasn't holding onto anything. I was flying through this world. Frantic and afraid. Blind without a clue as to how much I couldn't see.

I hated food.

I hated food because it was easier to hate than to face the hell I was walking straight into.

It was easier to hate than to love someone I was taught to despise.

Who would love me? Who could?

Chapter Seven

Just like the rain falling at my doorstep, I wish I could pull at the images of that day, those nights and watch them drift away.

Disappear into something unknown.

I wish I could forget the cold of your bicycle creeping through my pants as you brought me back to my place that night.

Or the way the tires skid over the snow as ice kissed the pavement.

I wish I didn't remember that goddamn apartment.

That mattress lying on the floor.

That room that barely belonged to you.

I wish I didn't know what it was like to rather throw myself at the cars zooming past than deal with the possibility of a life ruined, of a body in this much pain.

I didn't want this. I never did.

Chapter Eight

Looking out over the world,
scattered,
distant,
I've never felt so isolated
from it all.
I wonder
if anyone else feels like this?
A calming cold
looping itself around my lungs,
I stick my hand into the wind,
trying to hold on.
I wonder
if anyone else is reaching
out for me?

Chapter Nine

My fingers ran along the edges of the cracks in my body and I felt my confidence shred itself apart.

The crust chipping away as I moved them up and down,

I saw the months of progress burn underneath the layers I broke off in my hand.

Disgust wiped itself on my tongue – I gagged and found myself,

by coincidence?

by habit?,

hovering above my reflection.

It broke apart when I spit,

shattering the temptations

that lured my hands

up

instead of
down.
The scents
romanticized my memories
as my mind
        struggled
        to remain clear.
Pressing my forehead
on the bowl,
I inhaled the cold and it froze me still.
How did I let myself get here,
when I thought I'd come
so
far?

Chapter Ten

We ran through the streets with sweat rolling off our backs. Our fingers interlaced, we swerved through the crowds stopping to look up at this building and ducked under store awnings to avoid the occasional drops of rain.

The way our lungs seemed to rise and fall, the way our legs shook every time we stopped, made me think we wouldn't make it but once we saw the archway, I knew we would.

There were only a few minutes left of daylight and we looked at each other, then at the corner of Spring and Canal. Your eyes glimmered, the setting streaks of sun highlighting all the shades of brown I fell in love with so many years ago.

You shook your head, urging us forward, and

we sprinted across the intersection. Dodging car after car, leaving their honks in our wake, I thought we'd made it.

We were right there after all.
My right foot touched the sidewalk and I was about to bring up my left one.

But then I felt your hand jerk backwards and slip away. I couldn't hold on to your hand.
Something pulled you, took you from me.
I didn't understand.
Where had you gone? What happened?
I turned around and saw your body splayed on the crosswalk in front of a car ready to reverse and drive away.
Instead of going to you, I picked up the empty garbage can on the corner an-

"You okay?" Your words broke me from the world and I gripped your hand tight.
Together.

Chapter Eleven

She gripped her face and dug her fingernails in as deep as they'd go.

Trying to pull off the skin that still smelled like him.

Trying to tear off the nose that still remembered his shampoo.

Trying to rip out the hair that he pulled on.

But there were so many "hims" weren't there?

Too many?

When the memory of one fades,
another comes back in full color.

Chapter Twelve

How much am I worth? Do I have an amount on my forehead? Written in an ink only they can see.

I've scrubbed my face off but I still see them watching.

How much am I worth? Is it enough to feel like royalty? Or do I belong in the 99-cent bin?

Can someone tell me so I know how to feel? How to walk, how to sleep?

I don't know who I am if I don't know what I'm missing.

Can I make up the change that doesn't make me enough?

Am I 5 cents short or 5 million?

Can I save my tears and trade them in for points?

What can I do to make up the gap? Tell me and I'm yours.

Tell me and I'm whole.

Chapter Thirteen

Looking out,
all I see is a barrage of the moments I've run
from.
Thrashing against a current carrying me too
far from home.

A crash into these crowded walls.
Reaching for something stable amidst these
waves.
A body pinning mine to the floor.

The tide is strong,
it pulled me out more than once.
More than it should have.
More than I should have let it.

Chapter Fourteen

I will crush you,

under a weight I've tried to shed.

Your heart can't be safe with me --

no matter the prayers I've etched onto my

lips.

There is something else,

someone else,

rapping on the windows of my soul.

A devil disguised.

I have beaten it into a hibernation

I thought was forever.

But on nights,

nights where it smells like this,

I don't know how to keep it away.

*i don't want to go
without you*

Chapter Fifteen

Sometimes I think of you and I see him coming back for me.

Creeping out from the corners of a box I'd hammered shut long ago.

I think of you and I feel the goosebumps start to crawl up my arms. I can't feel anything but him anymore.

I can't even hear you.

I never wanted this from you.

Never wanted this at all but least of all from you.

Thinking of you never brought him out like this before. It never tainted my taste buds like this.

You were always a comforter I could wrap

myself in. The worn-in type I'd had since childhood.

But now he's here and that's gone. He burned it into ashes that he's since given me to hold. The remnants of an us I don't have anymore.

I wonder if we'll ever get that blanket back.

If we'll ever be able to create something new.

If we'll ever get a chance.

Chapter Sixteen

What would you have done
if I kissed you that night?
Under a canopy of cheap Christmas lights
and tattered tapestries,
Would you have pulled away?
From me, from all of this.
From what this would mean?
Or would you have leaned in?
Walked into the ocean with me?
We could have swam away. Far from the
things that made us tremble.
We could have found an island somewhere
in the middle of the Atlantic.
Made it our own.
Taken those traumas that screamed until we
fell asleep

and shed them with our clothes.
Nothing would seem out of control as long
as you held on to me
and I to you.

Your lips,
my lips
the worlds they could've healed --
if only they met that night.

Chapter Seventeen

Do you know what it feels like to not be able to get a mouth full of air? To have your breath stopped midway down your throat?

Stolen. Not in a romantic way.

Like an "oh my god, you've taken my breath away".

I would've preferred that. That way doesn't hurt like this. That way won't sting a month from now as I pull this memory from the back of the case it'll be packed in. And it won't burn on its way back down.

I would've rather died in ignorance than live like this. With this part of you exposed to me for the first time. Maybe it always was but I didn't see it.

I don't want to see it.

But now–
please.
I don't want to go without you.

Chapter Eighteen

Sometimes I'm glad I never got to say good-
bye to you.

It would have been too difficult. I'm scared I
would have stayed.

Shoved myself into the walls so that I'd
never have to leave.

I think I probably would have cried.

Too much, not enough.

For all the times we shared together.

For all the ways I both died and was born
within your walls.

For all the things that were taken
and that I took.

For all the love that grew and disappeared.

I miss you all the time but never more than

when I'm looking over your fences, so close but unable to touch.

I think that's the worst part. The thing that hurts me the most.

Seeing you happy with someone else, seeing another girl call you their home.

You were mine.

Chapter Nineteen

I am not enough. Of anything. For anyone.

Not enough.

My tongue is not familiar with Her words or Theirs.

I am balancing on this bridge between two worlds.

Two worlds growing further and further apart.

Testing the limits of the wood beneath my feet.

Splintering with every step I take.

Trying to find ways to make you want me, find ways to make them see me.

If I scream louder,

Will you hear me?

How long do I have to fight for you until you
open your arms to a traveler gone too long?
How many more miles must I walk,
how many more mountains should I scale,
move,
destroy
before you deem me worthy?
And what 'til then?
Where do I go?
Who do I say I am
when no one wants to claim this wayward
soul?

Chapter Twenty

Drawing only the slightest amount of blood, he struck her cheek and it lingered.

Lingered...

all she could visualize was the door slamming.

Over

and over again.

Closing on her face.

Slamming shut.

The echoes reverberating off the creaking walls and broken floor.

Stop.

She tried to stop the image.

Stop

It's not that day.

She tried to ground herself, find things to keep her feet steady in the present.

But things came too fast.

Her legs were already shaking, wobbly, unstable.

Unreliable.

Why resist?

Fall back into that day, that night. Those patterns, that year.

Embrace the splintered past.

"No."

> But since when did my 'no' mean anything?

Chapter Twenty-One

The other day, you were doing your daily, morning walk when they came up from behind and knocked you to your knees.

Today, you were heading to your car after a trip to ShopRite, and couldn't even get your keys out of your pocket before they smashed your head into the trunk.

Tomorrow, you will be bringing the trash in when they'll run and punch you so hard, you bounce right off the asphalt.

Next week, you won't be able to stop tasting your blood from the tongue you bit when they swung your body to the groun-

STOP.

I can't stop. My mind won't let me.

I blink, hard. Trying to escape these horror

movies, but no matter where I look, they're there.

They meet me in the dark to tear my dreams apart. They're the constant soundtrack in my mind, scraping at my ears until the blood clogs them shut.

I don't want to think these things so much that they become real, that they make their way into this world.

But they're here. They're here and I can't do anything to stop them.

So I see you, your faces, but I don't want to see you there, alone. I don't want to see you lifeless. I don't want to see these things at all.

I need to protect you.

I need to protect you.

I need to protect you.

How can I protect you?

Chapter Twenty-Two

For the longest time, I wanted to be exactly like him. I craved his respect, his admiration.

He liked this song? So did I.

He ate that? Me too.

He seemed carefree in a way even my five-year old mind wouldn't let me be. He never let me too close but the arms-length distance he held me at gave me just enough hope to always want more.

But then, on a single day, everything flipped. He suddenly became the face of everything I said I would never be.

The distance we existed at wasn't enough anymore. I needed space, more than what existed. I hated what we shared.

How come he got to break apart this house

like he did and still sleep under the same roof that same night? How was it possible to both hate someone so much and also still crave their acceptance?

I wanted in to whatever club he was apart of. I wanted him to want the same from me.

But the more he didn't, the more I let that hate eat up the love or whatever was left from those childhood years.

I have so many questions for him that I know will die unanswered. And I'm trying to figure out how to manage those frustrations coupled with a guilt I can't seem to shake.

One that tells me I gave up on him. That I never truly gave him the chance he deserves.

It whispers every night that we don't talk and keeps me in this fatigue. I don't want to hate him anymore but I also can't seem to figure out how to love him. How to love someone who does all the things that have killed me.

Someone who will never understand that.

Chapter Twenty-Three

I want to be enough. I want to stop searching for more, reaching for more. I want to settle into my skin and feel whole. I don't want to be afraid of being left alone. Of being left at all. If you're enough, that shouldn't matter. That shouldn't hurt. That shouldn't happen. But if it does, would it burn?

Chapter Twenty-Four

On days like today,
where the clouds cruise just out of reach,
where the skies drip with frost,
I remember those mornings in the car with
you.
It's funny,
thinking back,
seeing how much I spoke when
really
I never did say much, did I?

Chapter Twenty-Five

I don't want to miss you like this.

I want to miss you the way I miss the sun on those foggy days that come far too often.

I want to miss you the way I long for snow on a sunny day.

Sure that you will return.

That any day now we will be reunited as if the time apart

was actually no time at all.

But the way I miss you now,

I could have never dreamt of this.

Could have never dreamt of missing you in a forever type of way.

In a I-might-never-see-you-again type of way.

I never thought you would be my eclipse.

One day there but the next,
gone for a lifetime.

You were supposed to be stuck with me.
      Here for a lifetime of shooting stars.
You were never supposed to disappear.
      No one was supposed to disappear
again.
I don't want to miss you like this.
      I don't want to miss you at all.

Chapter Twenty-Six

I never wanted this. A world without you. I don't know if I'm in denial. If I'm tricking myself into seeing a future that'll never happen but in the depths of my mind.

But how am I supposed to imagine a future at all without us?

Without that pixelated video game and those sleepless, slaphappy nights?

Without those matching shirts and that music that still rings in my ears?

Without those early-morning-talks and those times you held my parts while I broke down beside you?

I've lost too much.

Haven't you?

Why do we need to lose anymore?

In a world that's taken so much away, don't you want to hang on tighter?

Stronger?

Harder?

I'm not letting go. I don't care if it's burning my hands right off. I'm not leaving this.

I'm not getting on that lifeboat unless you climb in with me.

Climb in with me.

you will always be safe with me

Chapter Twenty-Seven

I want your hair, tossed and damp, running their way through my fingers as we lay — heads resting on the pillows cradling our necks.

The sound of rain drops lightly tapping for our attention.

The wind pushing leaves into piles for us to jump into.

But nothing could take me away from you.

In this moment, those things are distractions from a world with you.

A world of cotton soft textures and silk-spun bedsheets.

It's a world free of the smoke that chokes us.

It's a world of endless wildflowers waiting for our arrival.

A chance to taste the ocean breeze as it crashes in our mouths. I could live here forever. Would you?

Chapter Twenty-Eight

I moved myself across the seas in search of a gold I always dreamed of.

But instead,

I found you.

I didn't understand why I hadn't found you sooner.

I could've saved everyone a lot of pain.

And wrecked ships.

And wasted blood.

I should've known better sooner, faster.

I should've known.

Chapter Twenty-Nine

It's so easy for me to get lost. I never mean to, I don't even want to, truthfully. For someone so afraid of so much, you'd think that wandering from the path in front of me wouldn't come as easily.

But it's like this:

I am with you and you slow down to take a Polaroid of a flower you can't help but sniff. I smirk, and keep my pace — slow, steady, just a couple of feet ahead. Ready for you to meet me.

But just as I hear your footsteps coming closer to mine, my body shivers. The shadows dancing just beyond the trail start to look taller, louder. Grotesque forms creeping in on us, I have to get out there to protect you from this. I can't let them touch you.

Touch us.

I have to keep you safe.

You will always be safe with me.

And then I'm gone and it's like I can't even remember what the sun feels like. Or how magical the light looks as it cuts through the brush. Or how far your laugh lifts me into the sky.

I'm fighting these monsters and I'm lost in this darkness. I try to blink them away but the more I do, the deeper I fall in.

I've grown so used to it by now, it doesn't feel like much of anything when I'm down there.

But it's that absence of life that pushes me back towards you.

Because I know that you are the one that keeps me safe. I close my eyes and there you are. I feel your hands rest on my shoulders, your breath warm the frost off my ears. Your body brings me back to reality and your heart beats mine awake. You give me the air my lungs need to resuscitate themselves, and I can smell the freshness of the forest again. I taste the morning dew. I can feel the coolness in the dirt beneath my shoes.

I am here. And the trees are just trees again. The shadows just that.

You ground me in a world more beautiful than I ever let myself see and for that and so much more, I take your hand and we continue forward. Just us, right here.

Chapter Thirty

The other night you brushed my toes with yours and my heart skipped two beats before returning to normalcy.

I felt that familiar shroud of secrecy fall over our shoulders.

We huddled together under the covers. Careful not to let them see we were there, we turned the flashlight off.

We giggled.

And it felt electric.

Like that time when you put your hand on my glasses and I swore I could've kissed you.

Should've kissed you.

It's that alleyway we've long abandoned in favor of the wide-open road.

That dance we don't have to do anymore.

The exhilaration of a secret. Stolen glances, careful laughs.

Our hands just a centimeter apart, a moment where they're not. The feel of your lips cuddled into mine, your chest moving up and down.

The warmth of a cover beneath locked doors.

The salvation in your hips.

It's like a step back in time but without that fear that this is wrong, or worse, that we might be.

It's the tightrope walk across these towers but with a safety net keeping us steady.

I didn't know I'd welcome this tip toe we'd have to do, but the next time you grab my hand, even for a moment, I hope you feel it too.

Chapter Thirty-One

I can taste our beginning as crisp as if it were yesterday. My heart is bouncing, jumping against my chest, as I think back to the days of being too scared to look at you.

Afraid that you'd know just through my eyes alone.

Afraid that you could tell of the dreams I'd had, of the way I held you then, of the ways you kissed me.

Each time I blinked, I felt my mind wander further and further from reality and talking to you soon seemed impossible.

How could I?

You could never know,

of course.

But I wanted you to.

Wanted to find out if these dreams I'd had were shared. If you too avoided my eyes out of fear, out of curious shame. Out of a desire to see if holding my hand would quell the shaking in your bones. The deep rattle that keeps you up at night with thoughts of a life that'll never be.

But that time- that was the first time I'd danced on a line so fine.

I didn't even know I could balance like that before.

We teetered on this tightrope for so long, my toes shook. Biting my nails wasn't enough anymore. Each moment that went by without you knowing pushed me closer and closer to the depths of a chasm I wanted to draw close.

You were just on the other side.

Or were you in the middle with me?

How I managed not to fall is one of the greatest mysteries of all time. Nancy Drew herself wouldn't be able to figure it out.

It's funny how clear those memories still are for me, almost six years later.

I close my eyes and there I am.

Letting go, wishing for you to catch me.

Chapter Thirty-Two

You light the world on fire for me.

I don't know how to keep this love contained.

From bursting through my pores.

From spilling from my mouth.

I am overwhelmed,

consumed,

in an instant and am not sure how to survive when it feels like I can't think of anything but your love.

See.

Breathe.

Feel.

Anything but you.

I love you so much.

Did you know that?

Know that some days all of a sudden it'll hit me like a punch to the throat. And I lose my breath.

Lose my ability to do anything but want to be wrapped in your arms,

wrap you in my arms.

Nothing can stop me from trying to tell you about the things I can barely put words to.

Chapter Thirty-Three

You danced on the walls around us,
Your hips slow and steady
Your voice flickering in the wind.
I couldn't look away. I still can't.
You put the room in amber as I rolled to my back to take you in.
I don't know why it's so easy for me to forget you, these nights, this place.
As if it means nothing.
As if I could truly forget.

Chapter Thirty-Four

Do you remember that day?

Because I can recall it like it was yesterday.

Our bare feet dancing amongst thick blades of grass, coarse and hard,

our toes sinking into the soil.

Dirt smushed underneath our arches,

puddles formed with every drop of rain that fell from that sky,

blue as the ocean just across the way,

blue as the sheets on that bed that opened me whole.

We splashed through each one as we ran around to the front of the house.

Screaming and laughing,

giggling as though we had just stolen a candy bar from the local corner store, giggling as if we didn't have a whole world waiting to tear us apart.

Because we didn't, in that moment, that week, we were allowed to just be. For the first time, we could just exist. In each other.

With each other.

Wild nights followed wild days. And we pushed our bodies further than they'd been as we reached peaks higher than we'd ever known existed.

So as we stood there, rain dripping down our backs, shirts soaked through, I saw the emerald in your eyes and forgot the cold that shivered up my spine. Forgot the world that was waiting just outside.

And existed.

Chapter Thirty-Five

You found me during a time in my life where I wasn't sure what was real and what wasn't.

You saw my reputation burn by both my own hand and theirs.

You saw them take turns spreading lies based in a truth that at times I wasn't sure existed and at others, was only a sliver of the story they didn't want to hear.

You heard me do more harm to myself than I'd ever done before, unsure how to sleep in the bed I'd made.

You felt my hate grow until it consumed me and still reached in to deliver the tiniest bit of hope.

You shut off your ears to the things they

tried to tell you and decided to stay even when I wasn't sure I should.

You held me when I let them take pieces of me I still can't get back.

You helped me fill in those spaces with pockets of gold.

You shook off the debris I was buried under and found air for me to breathe again.

You were there as I relearned how to walk, how to swim.

You cradled my heart until I was ready to give it a home where it would be safe to grow and hurt and thrive and love.

You made me want to show up for myself. You saw me when no one else did.

Sometimes I'm not sure how we got here, why you never left through a door I practically held open for you some nights. But regardless of the questions I still have, that I suppose I always will, you have held up a reflection of myself I don't want to shatter anymore.

And I will spend the rest of my life holding one up for you.

Chapter Thirty-Six

Eyes open, eyes closed.
What does it really matter?

This darkness isn't so overwhelming when
the sky
is filled with you.

Chapter Thirty-Seven

The way my lips curl around the letters of
your name,
   the way they slide over each curve with such
familiarity,
   they must have been made for this,
   made for you.

There's no other explanation for why they
fit so perfectly in my mouth.

   Each letter, the perfect shape.
   each sound, the perfect note.

It's no wonder
I can't stop screaming your name.

Chapter Thirty-Eight

I missed you.
It's been a while
since we spoke.
But don't worry, my love,
I'll always -
always -
have room for you.

Chapter Thirty-Nine

It's been some time since I could close my eyes and know that the world wouldn't hurt me.

That I'd be in a world all my own.

In fact, all I've known recently is fear so cold, so strong, it grips my throat tight.

Leaving their mark around my neck.

A reminder that they were the ones to steal the one thing keeping me afloat.

But the other night, as I woke for the third time, I rolled into you and felt its grip loosen. Air came slow.

But it came.

And you,

the smooth of your skin on mine,

you revived the heart in danger of giving in to the silence that drowned me twice before.

Until you threw that life vest onto me and pulled me in.

I still don't get a perfect night's rest but I wake now at least only to look at you.

Chapter Forty

Words exploding before they're said,
bombs dropping in my stomach.
How did we get here?
So far apart from one another.
Come back to me,
and stop this bleeding.
Heal my wounds,
our wounds,
and stop the gun from shooting.
Please.

Chapter Forty-One

You chose me? You choose me? Every day? Why? How?

How is it that out of all the people out there that love you,

out of all the people out there that could, that you are here with me in this moment?

That you roll over each morning and take a look at my sleep-ridden face, groggy and lined by the marks of the pillows and blankets I hog, and think "I choose her, always"?

Do you know what knowing this does to me? The ways it makes me question everything I've ever known? The ways it makes me think about the love I never knew until that day you held my face still enough to fix the broken glasses balancing on my nose?

You choose me, I choose you. Always.

Chapter Forty-Two

We soak in silence,
absorbing the melodies
of our breath
as the sun cuts across the room,
illuminating a magic
invisible to everyone
but us.

Chapter Forty-Three

Your hands are tender
raw,
as you try to carry love,
cradling lost hearts
in search of their owners.
Never resting,
they are soft,
so soft,
from wounds
not given the chance
to heal.

Chapter Forty-Four

In my drunken stupor,

I saw you standing there before me so clear and steady.

The room spun and soon my mind would black out

but as your face approached mine,

the music seemed to quiet.

I wished desperately to keep myself sentient just long enough to remember

how it'd feel.

Chapter Forty-Five

I was rinsing my plate
when you wrapped your wings
around my waist
and tickled my ear with your feathers.
Turning, I shook water in your face
and your hands
brought out the sun
in my mouth.
As you flew away,
I felt your song
kiss my lips goodnight

Chapter Forty-Six

Today I opened my mouth
and swallowed all the clouds
that swirled around your face,
your figure.
They were soft on my tongue,
light and airy.
Just as I had imagined they'd be.

Chapter Forty-Seven

Counting the hairs on my arms,
I never realized how many of them there are.
How close together they live,
lying in parallel,
rarely touching.
I like to lay them flat.
Only for you to make them stand.

Chapter Forty-Eight

This is the only thing that has saved me,
that has saved my mind.

My salvation, my grace.

You are the sun setting over the hills we stand on.

You are the fog settling into its place for the night.

You are it.

All of it.

Chapter Forty-Nine

I remember sitting on the sidewalk. Legs scrunched together, pebbles rolling by.

The fake cigarette blowing sugary smoke from the other end. The pretzel sticks jutting out of my pocket.

I pictured a ladder swinging from my bedroom window to yours.

A can with string we could share secrets through.

Two clouds of sugar circling our heads.

But the breeze cut deep at that time of day and I felt the sun pierce my heart.

Reminding me that you're still out there, a world, and then some, away.

Chapter Fifty

I want your arms around my shoulders, a cape keeping me steady in the air.

40,000 feet above the world that towered over us. Nothing matters when we're this high.

Can we get away again?

You and me to the stars, the galaxy.

Let's ski down the Milky Way and swim in the black lagoons of the sky.

Let's surf the asteroids and sunbathe on the moon.

Can't we get away from all this noise?

Create our own symphony of chaos and color?

We don't need the northern lights – we can make our own.

Chapter Fifty-One

I've dreamed of a love so potent I never thought I'd survive its journey into my heart.

I wanted something breathtaking, stomach dropping. I wanted you before I knew a love for me existed.

Before I knew I deserved a love at all.

I wanted you in a hundred thousand hours before bed when I prayed for a way to survive these nights of pain.

I wanted you forever with every breath and every whisper.

With every beat of my heart.

I thought I wouldn't be lucky enough to find you, to love you, but I wanted you. And I wanted to give you the chance to want me too.

And maybe this want was a need or maybe this want wasn't just desire.

Or maybe the desire grew so grand it eclipsed the universe and brought me to you.

But now I lay here and open my eyes and I've never stopped wanting the chance to want you.

Chapter Fifty-Two

Cries of longing from an ocean away.
When will I find you, my love?
When will you find me?

Chapter Fifty-Three

I want to hold you, to take your hand in mine, and bring you into my chest.

I want to hold you, to wrap my arms around your shoulders, to be your safe harbor from the world.

I want to hold you, to carry you through these fires, and let you rest gently through the night.

I want to hold you, to run my fingers through your hair, to catch the tears before they fall.

But something took my body within its grasp
and told me I wouldn't get that chance.
You wouldn't get that comfort you need.

Something took me and no matter how hard I thrashed, it never let go. Its hold too strong — so strong.

It convinced me that holding you would only hurt you.

That my touch,
my hands,
my body,
brought pain.

And you had had enough of that, so I listened.

For so long, I listened,

I bowed in obedience to this something I was too afraid to look at.

But it's been too many days like this, and you need me now. So I'm going to rip away at this straight jacket they threw on me, I'm going to tear through the wires keeping me from you, and I will be there.

I don't know how long I'll be, I don't know what I'll be like when I get there, but please,

please,
trust that I'm coming.

Trust that I will hold you into the night and
tomorrow.

Chapter Fifty-Four

The stars danced on your shoulders last night,

before bouncing into my eyes.

I was struck in that moment —

by the light they brought from you to me.

Do you know the brightness you hold?

This airy, iridescent shade of brilliance the world sees.

Do you see it too?

I hope so but I don't think so.

I think you might be the one who needs glasses now,

because I see everything.

I see each color as the sun passes over your eyes in the morning,

each shade as the moon illuminates your
body,
each curve its own work of art.
You — art in and of itself.
Do you want to take the blinders off,
the ones they forced upon your eyes?
It's probably going to hurt —
they've spent decades stuck in place after
all.
But I promise when you see what I see,
when you see what we see,
you will never be able to look away.

she had something to say

Chapter Fifty-Five

i used to think i cried alone.
that when my tears kissed the ground,
they dried up in silence.

never heard, never seen, never known.

but today,
today i hear the sounds of us all.

our cries together —
they ring in my ears,
in their ears.

we're not alone, it seems,
our ancestors are screaming with us.

Chapter Fifty-Six

I fell asleep the other night

and in an instant, I was back on that plane five years ago.

And all I could feel was a fear and excitement keeping me awake.

All I can see is the journey I took alone that summer.

That move.

That unknown leap into a pit of nothingness.

A darkness with no bottom.

I had no idea that when my toes would reach the soil,

they'd be covered in flowers.

Wild. Untamed.

I'm ready for another.

Chapter Fifty-Seven

It took me a long time,
Longer than I'd like to admit,
to drop the towel and stand there,
    naked,
in front of a mirror.
No filter, no armor.
No soft glow, no perfect angles.
Just you, her.
    Me.
Kicking the towel to the side,
I finally feel her clear the pit retaining all
that water, all those tears.
I'm so much lighter,
I hold onto the counter so I don't fly away.
    "Finally."

Chapter Fifty-Eight

The first time someone called me a whore, and not in the joking-late-90s-early-2000s-politically-incorrect kind of way, I was in my late teens. This boy who I had been spending time with one summer said that he had "heard" from someone that I was a whore, slutty, crazy.

That I "slept around"

and at the time, I laughed it off. Laughed about how lame they must be.

Laughed about how "wrong" they were.

But that night, I remember crawling deep into my bed,

wrapping myself in the flannel sheets and biting them hard,

hoping that if I exerted enough effort,

enough strength,

that would break the shame that struck me.

Why couldn't I escape this past I knew was filled with mistakes

both of my own making and not?

Had I not run far enough?

Fast enough?

Wasn't I allowed to fuck up too?

Or was it just them? Just him? And him? And her? And them?

I traveled hundreds of miles away to escape you and yet there you were.

"You can't escape me," you whispered, sly, sexy. You sure had a way of tricking me into believing you were right.

It would take a lot more running away, broken legs, broken bones, before I shook you out of my head. And you're still not gone.

Not totally.

But I have enough of my voice back to know the truth from your lies.

To know the warmth of forgiveness after leaving her stuck in that cold for far too long.

Chapter Fifty-Nine

I organized the first kiss I ever had with a girl.

The first time I let my lips travel where they wanted to, not where they were trained to.

It was short. And in a room full of teenage boys I couldn't have cared less about.

I knew there wouldn't be a chance to do this again.

And in that one second, I knew something had been ignited but it was growing too fast.

It was growing too hot.

I didn't think this would happen.

That I'd be branded in that instant. Scarred with a teasing temptation to find out more.

So I doused myself in whatever was in the fire extinguisher out back and I really thought

I'd extinguished it after that night. Fixed myself. Put out the flames that kept me up at night.

I was what? Sixteen? Seventeen?

I should've known better.

You can't put out a four-alarm fire with a fire extinguisher.

You just have to let it take you and

burn. you. alive.

Chapter Sixty

You brought your cross down on my head
and knocked me to my knees.
You said it was
for my own good.
I think you might
have even
cried.
Or maybe that was the
holy water
I drowned in
or the blood from the whips
lashing across my back
You used to have a
halo.
You were as close to a saint as there could
be.

But now I see your wings
for what they are.
Extensions of a hate baked into
the body and blood you drink,
So keep at it.
At least one of us
will be remembered for love.

Chapter Sixty-One

I don't want fame and recognition only when I die. I don't want to spend a whole year putting pen to paper, a whole life, with nothing to show for it. What good would that do?

Praise post-mortem. Too late for me.

Just in time for them

but fuck them.

Who are they anyway? Why do they get to pat themselves on the back years after I'm no longer around to accept the congratulations?

Why is my success not in my own hands?

Are these not my own words? My stories? My blood?

They shouldn't get to decide my place, in history, if any place at all. I'm not sure why it's

taken me this long to get to this point if I'm be-
ing honest.

I've never liked listening to what others had
to say. Craft my life around their terms.

So why would I cave on this? Why would I
let someone else tell me whether or not talent
lives in these lines?

I know there's something there and it's my
choice to find it or leave it hidden. Mine.

Not theirs, not anyone's.

Not anymore.

Chapter Sixty-Two

Tears fall faster and faster as
I sit,
a million miles away,
across a white desert,
reaching out across the void,
hoping to find you.
Your sobs are carried by the wind
closer, closer,
they bounce off the walls in my head as I
rush to your side, to find nothing,
no one.

Powerless, useless.
No words of mine will soothe the wounds
you lick.
My touch only brings more splinters.

I am sorry.
My heart falls
but I continue running
in search of you,
a cure for you.

Chapter Sixty-Three

Heavy.

What does that even mean?

Like weights stacked on top of my chest?

Like the baggage I've carried hanging off my shoulders?

Yes.

No?

I'm not really sure anymore.

I know that it means something I don't like anymore.

I know that it means something that reminds me of years long gone now.

A time I don't want to go back to.

So I guess that's where I'm at.

Feeling h e a v y.

Air can flow in and out of my mouth and I will still feel heavy.

I walk around and my feet drag under who I feel I've become.

What am I doing to myself? To everyone around me? Who have I become? Who have I let myself become? Where --

I don't want to finish that question because I know what I was going to say and I am not going back there.

I am not going back to where I was.

I am not going back.

I can't.

I won't get out this time.

Can't I just live with it? With you?

Live with the grey skies shifting back and forth,

live with the heaviness dropped onto my back,

live with the cuts that never healed,

live with the throbbing in my feet.

~~I am heavy.~~

No.

I *feel* heavy. I *feel* heavy.

Heaviness.

Chapter Sixty-Four

I wish I had your skin under my fingernails,
your hair still resting on mine.

I wish I could pull your words out from inside my ears

And play them for the world to hear.

I wish I could let them taste the shame that keeps me quiet

And the guilt that beats me down.

I wish I could show them the things I can't unsee

and make them feel your hands on my wrists,

the weight of your body on mine on top of your twin bed.

Make them watch me say no

And witness the moment I realized that wasn't enough.

Have them listen to the doubt

trying to stop my fingers from even typing

what no one will ever read.

I wish I could wear those blood-stained sheets,

the ones you said you'd wash so no one would know,

the ones that made me Google

if it was normal to bleed like I did.

To leave so much of myself on that bed

for you to get rid of.

For me to search for.

Maybe then I wouldn't be shaking at the thought

of sharing this with someone other than myself.

Maybe then I wouldn't be imagining the million things

in my past that they'd use against me,

that they'd use to protect you.

Maybe then I'd be able to let the past go

and experience what healing feels like.

Chapter Sixty-Five

Nights like these remind me of us. Shivering, teeth chattering. These were the times I'd crawl to you.

On my hands and knees, scraping against the black-ice-covered asphalt. There I'd go. Back to your door.

Sealed tight, you always opened it for me.

Even if I stumbled in,

even if I never remembered you the next day.

Even if I yelled and cried for you to just leave me alone, you never turned me away for good.

It's been a while since I've seen you.

I hope time has treated you well.

I hope that door is welded shut for good.

Chapter Sixty-Six

I biked to the woods with a flashlight in my waistband and a backpack full of snacks. The quick ride over flew almost as fast as my thoughts.

What were we going to do first? Find the palette stacked against those trees?

Build a bridge to traverse the brook?

Fashion a rope swing to toss us far and wide?

In there, amongst the dead leaves and quenched soil, the world seemed warm.

It was ready for me. It wanted me.

It wanted these adventures brewing in the soles of my feet.

It gave me a freedom to dream, gave me the space to breathe.

This was before the hims and hers.

The thems and their hushed whispers and loud cackles.

This was when the sun shone on my shoulders and carried me home to you.

Chapter Sixty-Seven

I see her, calling to me. Reaching closer and closer until it's time for me to leave.

I hear her desperate, yearning screams dissipating into a calm I never once thought I'd hear.

We collided and broke into each other.

A cataclysmic episode neither of us survived.

I swore it'd be different this time.

That I'd come to you with all the force of a thousand tides.

And you'd welcome me home with just as much.

Our waves crashing into one another. We wouldn't be afraid anymore.

Not of the sea,

of it's endless depths,

of each other's.

We would melt into one another, together again at last.

Chapter Sixty-Eight

You're not so scary anymore you know. You used to be the thing of nightmares.

This blackness I couldn't get rid of.

You used to tempt me with your colors; so inviting and warm.

Only to throw me down and never let me up.

You stole my breath too many times for me to count and I swore that that would be the last time I'd let you in like that.

"I can't be your fool," I said. "Not anymore."

But I didn't see you then. I didn't understand what you, what we, could be.

Today I feel the power in my voice and scream so loud you'll never forget me.

Will you come to me now?

Now that I've learned to love you?

Chapter Sixty-Nine

The last time I was in the hospital I could barely get my name out of my mouth. The world spun faster than my legs could run and I just wanted everything to stop.

The words coming out of their mouths,

the voicemails on my phone,

the pounding in my temples.

I wanted the bad decisions and desperate choices to lead me down a road where the nurse wasn't saying I would be okay. I didn't want okay. I wanted an ending that was more final than that.

Lying in this room today, I see her. Not that nurse from so many years and nights ago.

But her. You.

A pain wrapping itself around your neck. A snake slithering it's way into your soul.

I see you. I see your blood spilt even if they don't. I see the way your heart breaks, over and over and over again.

I used to want to forget you. Pretend like you don't exist. After all, if I can't remember you, then you're not real.

You were never real, right?

But now — being here, seeing you lying there, I need you to know that I would take your hand if I could. Hold it in mine and squeeze it until you felt me in your corner. You always had someone in your corner. I never want you to be alone again.

Chapter Seventy

I still hear that voice. A him. A her. A them.
Why are you calling to me? For me?
I told you you're not welcome here.
Find someone else to be your home.
But those words, their words
— they shriek.
They scrape against the windows,
crawl their way into my mouth
until suddenly I can't tell them apart from mine.
Again.
Tricking me into more pain than I can handle.
Agai-
No. Stop it.
Please.

I don't deserve the things you whisper
I don't want them.
No one does.

Chapter Seventy-One

I took a deep breath in and winced, on instinct, but the pain never showed.

It still surprises me that I can do that.

That my bones don't break quite as easily as they used to.

I never thought this day would come. Truth be told, I never wanted it to.

If I'm not in constant danger of suffocation, what will my life become? I'd grown so attached to this idea of an us that I didn't stop to think about what forever would be like without that constant threat.

And more than that, than anything, was the fear that without that dance, I'd grow complacent, still.

Not in a way that would give me the clarity

and insight into a future unknown. But rather, a plateau barren and devoid of anything worth coming out of this pen of mine.

Now that I'm here though, what I see could not have widened my eyes further. My mouth is never closed, my jaw constantly agape.

Did you know that this day would come? Is that why you tried so hard to keep it away?

You knew that at first sight, I'd fall so deeply in love, the memories of us would fade and I'd finally learn to swim.